LITTLE BOOK FOR BiG CHANGES

STUDIO PRESS

The authors have researched the topics discussed in this book and relied on advice from people who are experienced in these subject areas. So far as the authors are aware, the information given is correct and up to date at the time of publishing, but should not be relied upon for professional advice.

The activities have been tested, but outcomes cannot be guaranteed. Some of the activities require adult supervision and assistance. While safety precautions have been noted throughout the book, ultimately readers have the responsibility to use this book in a safe and responsible manner.

The authors and publisher disclaim, as far as the law allows, any liability arising directly or indirectly from the use or misuse, of the information and activities contained in this book.

First published in the UK in 2018 by Studio Press,
an imprint of Kings Road Publishing, part of Bonnier Books UK,
The Plaza, 535 King's Road, London, SW10 0SZ
www.studiopressbooks.co.uk
www.bonnierbooks.com

Copyright © Karen Ng and Kirsten Liepmann
Illustrated by Simona Karaivanova

1 3 5 7 9 10 8 6 4 2
0280918

ISBN 978-1-78741-480-8

Printed in Malaysia

LiTTLe BooK FoR BiG CHANGES

activities and tips to make the world a better place

Karen Ng and Kirsten Liepmann

This book would not have been possible without Simona Karaivanova's wonderful and playful illustrations. We are grateful for your eternal patience with our numerous edits and your boundless creativity to bring our book to life.

Thank you, Tina Dubois, our agent at ICM Partners, and Emma Drage, our editor at Studio Press, for your confidence in our book's potential to inspire young readers. Your insights and guidance through the world of publishing have been invaluable.

We are grateful to all the individuals who took the time to review and provide feedback on our book: Lisa Apperly; Wendy Arnold; Dr Elizabeth Doherty, MD; Wendy Ernst; Dr Kristine M. Gibson, MD; Inés Lucia Fernandez; Joanna Heywood; Bryant Jew; Dr Claire Liepmann, MD; Lorraine Liepmann; Christine Ma-Lau; Marissa Moran; Gabriel Ng; Dr Daksha Patel, MD; James Di Paolo; and Neil Yeoh. We admire your efforts in addressing global challenges.

Our book started as a small project on Kickstarter and we owe a special thanks to those who helped to elevate our campaign: Tamsyn Brewster, Sophie Deen, Louis Huynh, Maria Springer and Faith Teo. We also must thank Sofia Brewster-Fox, Finn Byrne and Tobin Cooper, whose joy and curiosity upon reading some early drafts continued to drive our work.

We cannot even begin to list all of the friends and family who have supported us in creating this book, but we are so appreciative of having each of you in our lives.

Nobody has been more instrumental in the making of this book than our parents and role models: Stanley and Gloria Ng, and Holger and Lorraine Liepmann. Since we were young, you have shown us the importance of empathy, the power of action and the responsibility we share to take care of our world.

DEDICATION

This book is dedicated to our 409 Kickstarter backers,
who believed in this project from the very beginning
and helped to grow it beyond what we had ever imagined.

Thank you for thinking the world can be a better place
and that this little book can bring some big changes.

CONTENTS

PEOPLE

COMMUNITY

I ♥ Nature!

PLANET

WELCOME

Our world is pretty amazing: from the people that fill it, to the communities we build in it, to the planet itself! And **you** are a part of it all!

Let's be honest, though, our world is not perfect. It is facing many challenges and there are many ways that we can work to improve it. We are sure that you can already think of a few! These challenges are big and complicated, so they do not have easy solutions. Since they affect all of us, let's call them **global challenges**.

We are all a part of this world and we all need to help take care of it. You do not have to wait until you are older to help. Children can make a **big** difference, sometimes even bigger than grown-ups!

What have you noticed about our world that could use some improvement?

What do you want to do to make our world a better place?

Write or draw it here:

This book has fun activities and ideas to get you started. You will learn a bit more about some of these global challenges and find ways to help solve them. You will need grown-ups and friends to join you for a few of the activities.

Together, we can make big changes to improve our world!

GUIDE FOR GROWN-UPS

Dear Grown-ups,

Thank you for exploring complex world challenges with our young readers! Your involvement will make this book more meaningful. It will help children to engage with concepts at a deeper level and connect them to the real world. To support your efforts, we have outlined our goals, approach and some tips for your participation.

Goals

Global challenges are complicated, abstract and ever-evolving. Therefore, we do not aim to write a comprehensive book about each one. We use concrete examples and hands-on experiences focused on specific aspects of each challenge to help children begin to understand them. Consider this book as a first step to stimulate children's curiosity to learn more and stir their sense of responsibility.

Approach

In order to be motivated and prepared to make positive change, people need to feel connected to and responsible for the wider world. They need to be able to reflect and think critically about complex topics. And for that to happen, they need to be informed.

Our approach is inspired by the Learn-Think-Act framework used in Oxfam's global citizenship education material. Each chapter has activities designed for these stages, which we have interpreted as follows:

- **Learn:** Children are introduced to keywords, concepts and basic information on the current situations and causes relevant to the global challenges.
- **Think:** Children are prompted to think empathetically and creatively, ask questions and reflect upon their roles in their community and wider world.
- **Act:** Children are motivated and supported to take concrete actions around them – whether they are large or small.

Tips

The activities require varying degrees of adult supervision; from none to very hands-on. Of course, this will vary by child, so we recommend you check in and offer support as needed. Here are a few tips:

- **Preview:** Flip through the book to acquaint yourself with the activities, content and some potentially advanced vocabulary for which some children may need additional explanation.
- **Ask and discuss:** Ask children questions about what they read and the activities they have done. Talk about the concepts, support their curiosity and encourage them to ask questions, too.
- **Empathise:** Cultivate empathy – discuss how the topics make children feel and help them to explore different perspectives.
- **Connect:** Help to tie the concepts to what children see or experience around them as well as to current world events.
- **Model:** When children ask questions you cannot answer, work together to learn more and model how one can find information.

At the end of the book, we have provided a list of Resources and References for further learning. We hope you and the little global citizens in your lives enjoy exploring this book – and the world – together!

Karen and Kirsten

EXTREME POVERTY

Let's end poverty for people around the world!

Life can be full of ups and downs. Sometimes, it can take a lot of effort to get past challenges. Some people face extra challenges because they live in **poverty**. When people are living in poverty, it can be hard for them to get what they need to live safe and healthy lives.

Poverty also makes it harder for people to follow their dreams. They must make tough decisions about what they can buy and do.

What are things that you **want** to have in life? What are things that you actually **need** to survive?

Wants vs Needs

Think about things that you like. Decide if they are things that you want or things that you need. Draw, write or cut out images from magazines to fill in the table below:

THINGS I WANT	THINGS I NEED

What if some of your needs were taken away?

How would your life change?

GLUE

LIVING IN POVERTY

Many people in all parts of the world live in extreme poverty. This means they are surviving on less than about £1.40 a day. With little money, they often struggle to afford basic needs such as food and shelter.

There are many reasons why people are poor. For example, some people live where natural disasters, diseases or wars make it difficult for them to go to school or work. Some others fall into poverty because they lose their job or cannot find work because of what they look like or where they are from.

Try this activity to understand what everyday challenges extreme poverty can cause:

Poverty Line Challenge

Feed your family with only £1.40 a day per person for 3 days.

1) Calculate your **budget**, which is the total amount of money you are allowed to spend.
2) Go to the supermarket and find food items that you can afford. Write down their prices on the shopping list.
3) Using only the food you bought, come up with ideas for your family's breakfasts, lunches and dinners.

Discuss with your family:
- Did everyone feel they had enough to eat?
- Could you buy enough nutritious food with this budget?
- Imagine if £1.40 per day also had to pay for clothes, housing, transportation and medicine. How would this change things?

SHOPPING LIST

Budget: 3 days x £1.40 x .... = £ ....
Number of family members

Food items	Prices
....	....
....	....
....	....
....	....
....	....
Total cost	£

POVERTY TRAP

Being poor is more than not having enough to spend and going to bed hungry. It may also lead to other problems, such as poor health and little education. These can trap people in poverty for long periods of time, sometimes over many generations.

Some people can change this situation by not giving up and having strong support from family or friends. But many times this is not enough and outside help is needed. **Play this game to explore some poverty traps and ways to escape them:**

Poverty's Snakes and Ladders

You will need:
- A die
- A few small items to use as playing pieces

Play the game
1) All players put their pieces in box 1.
2) Take turns rolling the die to see how many spaces you move.

3) If you land on the head of a snake, you hit a poverty trap! Slide down to the bottom of the snake. If you land at the bottom of a ladder, you found a way to escape a poverty trap! Move to the top of the ladder.
4) The first player to reach the final box wins!

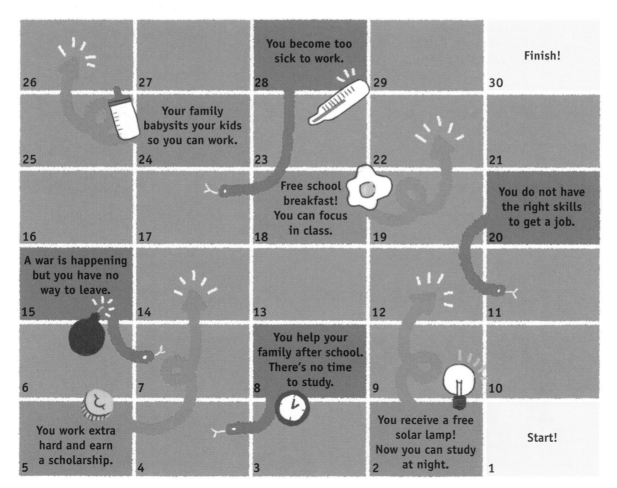

WHAT ELSE CAN YOU DO?

It's not easy for people to escape from poverty on their own. Luckily, people around the world are working together to end poverty. More governments are helping people who often need extra support, like children, the elderly and people with disabilities. Better education and work opportunities also help reduce poverty.

We are starting to see improvements – far fewer people are living in extreme poverty now compared to twenty years ago. But we still have a long way to go, as millions of people are still extremely poor.

You can help to end poverty for people around the world!
Here are a few ideas to get you started:

Learn More

- How many people live in extreme poverty today?
- In what areas of the world are there high numbers of people living in poverty?
- What is your government or community doing to help end poverty?

Engage Your Community

- Start a savings club with your friends. Ask grown-ups to share tips on how to save and spend money wisely.
- Organise a clothing swap with your neighbours so you do not have to buy new ones too often.

Donate and Volunteer

- Bring blankets and toiletries to a homeless shelter.
- Donate your birthday! Instead of gifts, ask friends to give money to a local charity.

Show Kindness

- Treat people the same way no matter how much money they have.
- Share your toys and games with others.

Can you come up with other ways to help?

UNIVERSAL EDUCATION

Let's make sure every child gets a good education!

Good education is one of the most powerful ways we can make our world a better place. **Education** is how we gain knowledge so that we can understand our world better and take care of it. It helps us to learn about each other, improve people's lives and reach our dreams!

Everyone should be able to have a good education. This means having things like books, helpful teachers and safe places that let everyone learn. But millions of children around the world do not get the opportunity to learn because of poverty, wars or unfair rules about who is allowed to go to school. **Explore what else can stand in the way of a good education with this activity:**

Obstacles to a Good Education

Talk with a grown-up and your teachers to find a good time to try this out!
Take on one challenge at a time and see how it might affect your ability to learn.

SOME CHILDREN...
live far from school or have no transportation to get there.

have few or no school supplies.

have no electricity at home or in school.

must work or help to take care of their families.

CHALLENGE YOURSELF AND...
wake up early and take a 20-minute walk before you go to school.

use only one pencil for a whole week.

do not use anything electronic at home (including lights, phones or computers).

do all the house chores, help make dinner and take care of your family before you study.

Imagine if you faced these challenges every day.

How would they affect your education?

16

EDUCATION AND GIRLS

Some children face extra challenges to go to school. Often, girls are at a disadvantage. In some places, families do not have enough money for all of their children to go to school. They choose to send boys but keep girls at home to work. Some families think it is fine for girls to marry early and drop out of school. In some areas, girls are not safe travelling to school or in the classroom.

Their schools may also be unclean, without private toilets or running water.

Educating girls will help them to improve their lives and their community. It can help to lower poverty, improve health and open more doors to education for everyone.

A New Story

Imagine a girl who is not going to school. Come up with ideas on how to change that, so she gets a good education. Write a new story for her!

_____

_____

_____

Why is she not going to school?

What changes need to happen so she can go to school?

_____

_____

What does a good education look like for her?

How does her life change because of her education?

_____

SCHOOL

POWER OF LITERACY

Do you remember when you first learned to read? If you can read and write, you are **literate**. Even though it can be hard at first, it is very important to be literate. One of the main ways that we communicate, share stories and gain new information is through reading and writing. People who are literate do better in school and have more job choices when they grow up.

Without access to a good education, many people in the world never have the chance to become literate.

Books and stories are great ways to learn and develop a love of reading. **Be a buddy and help someone to improve their reading skills!**

Reading Buddies

1) Find your buddy. Maybe it is a younger sibling, a friend or a grandparent. Learn about your buddy's interests and find a book that he or she would enjoy.
2) Get together for 15-20 minutes in a spot that's quiet enough for you to read together.
3) When you're together, try these different ideas:
   - Read out loud to your buddy.
   - Let your buddy read out loud. Help out when he or she has trouble with a word or sentence.
   - Read out loud together: say the words at the same time.
   - Take turns: you read a sentence or paragraph, then let your buddy read one.
   - Sit together but read in silence. You can even read different books!
4) Share what you each think about what you read. Can your buddy tell you what happened in the story?
5) Agree upon when you can get together again!

What else can you help someone to learn or practise?

WHAT ELSE CAN YOU DO?

Education improves people's lives and the world around us. People and governments have been working hard to make education better and available to all. Today, most children around the world enrol in primary school, and more are attending secondary schools and universities.

New technology and the Internet are helping to bring information to students who may not have got it easily before. In many places, there are still children who are being left out from education opportunities. Many children go to school, but they do not learn to read or do maths well.

You can help to make sure every child gets a good education!
Here are a few ideas to get you started:

Learn More

- What areas of the world have the most children who are not in school?
- What opportunities are there to learn outside of school?
- What can adults do to keep on learning?

Engage Your Community

- Set up a free book exchange, where people can leave their old books and pick up ones they have not yet read.
- Learn about programmes outside of school that help children learn.

Donate and Volunteer

- Hold a school supply drive to donate materials like pencils and notebooks to schools in need.
- Help younger children with their schoolwork.

Show Kindness

- Make a thank-you card for your teacher and others who help you to learn.
- Encourage classmates who are having a hard time with schoolwork to keep trying.

Can you come up with other ways to help?

HUNGER AND NUTRITION

Let's make sure everyone has enough nutritious food to eat!

When you haven't had enough to eat, have you ever felt tired, achy or even grumpy? Food gives us energy to run and learn. It is also full of **nutrients**, the building blocks that we need to grow and fight off illness. Proper nutrition is important to help children reach their ideal height and weight.

Millions of people around the world suffer from **malnutrition**, which means they are not getting enough food or all of the nutrients they need. This can cause serious health problems for children, like making their muscles and bones weak. It can also get in the way of paying attention and being active.

What are some of the key nutrients we need each day?

Unscramble the words to find out!

c _ b _ h y _ _ _ _ s
t b y a r e r c h o s d a

Get this energy-giving nutrient from brown rice and wholegrain bread.

p _ _ t _ _ n
e n p i t o r

To help build and repair your muscles, find this in meat, fish, nuts and eggs.

g _ _ _ f _ t _
d o g o s a f t

Found in oils, fish and avocados, these give energy and help to absorb vitamins.

i _ _ _
r o n i

We get this from meat, beans and green veggies to keep our blood healthy.

v _ _ _ m _ _ D
t i m a n i v D

To help build bones, get this from fish oil, eggs or even sunlight.

c _ l _ _ _ m
u l a c c i m

Dairy products have a lot of this to build strong bones.

LEFTOVER CHEF

About one third of food that is good enough to eat is wasted or lost each year. Some is lost during harvest, transportation or storage. But a lot is simply thrown away! Eating **leftovers** is a good way to avoid wasting food. There are many ways to turn leftovers into something new and delicious that everyone will enjoy!

Put on your chef's hat and try your hand at this clever leftover recipe from Peru! Grab a grown-up and get cooking!

Tacu Tacu

Ingredients
1 cup of leftover beans
1/2 cup of leftover rice
2 tablespoons cooking oil
1 clove garlic, crushed
1/4 teaspoon chilli paste
1/4 small onion, chopped

Preparation

1) Mash the beans in a bowl with a fork. Mix it with the rice by hand.
2) Heat 1 tablespoon of oil in a pan over a medium heat.
3) Add the garlic, onion and chilli. Cook for 3-5 minutes.
4) Remove from heat, let it cool, and then mix it with the rice and beans by hand.
5) Shape the mixture into two pancakes by hand. Each pancake should be about 10 cm across.
6) Heat 1 tablespoon of oil over a high heat and brown the pancakes in the pan until heated through (about 2 minutes per side).

Come up with your own leftover recipe!

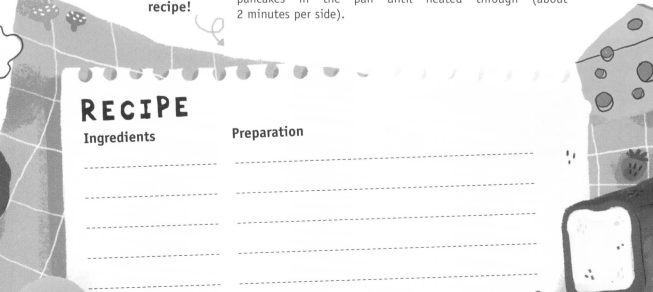

RECIPE

Ingredients

Preparation

SHARING FOOD

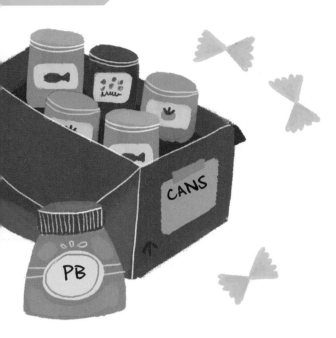

Did you know that there is actually enough food on Earth to feed everyone? So, why are there people who are malnourished or hungry?

Food waste is not the only problem. Wars and natural disasters like droughts can destroy farmland and food can be ruined when it is transported or stored. Local farmers may not grow healthy foods, stores may not carry them or some people may not have enough money to buy them.

A **food drive** is a way to collect food and **donate**, or give, it to those in need. **Organise a local food drive to help everyone in your community get the nutritious food they need.** Talk with a grown-up and gather some friends to help out!

Organise a Food Drive

Make a plan
Who?
Pick a local food organisation. See if it has advice about food drives.

What?
It is best to donate food that will not go bad quickly. Use what you know about nutrition to make suggestions.

Where?
Find a place where donations can be left, such as your school or home.

When?
Choose when to start and end the food drive.

How?
One way is to set out a large box where people can drop off donations.

Hold the drive
1) Make posters for the food drive that include the Who, What, Where, When and How.
2) Tell your family, friends, neighbours and teachers. Be ready to explain why it is important that they donate food.
3) At the end of the food drive, thank everyone who helped and donated. Deliver the food to the organisation you are supporting.

WHAT ELSE CAN YOU DO?

There is enough food for everyone in the world, but people are malnourished because food is wasted or not available to them. The good news is that we are finding smarter ways to grow and share our food. Some countries encourage farmers to grow crops so people can get more balanced nutrition.

There are governments and charities that run school breakfast programmes to get healthy food to children who do not get enough at home. Even though we are making progress, there are still too many people who are suffering because they are not eating enough safe and nutritious foods.

You can help to make sure everyone has enough nutritious food to eat! Here are a few ideas to get you started:

Learn More
- What areas of the world have the most people living with hunger?
- Where is the food you buy grown or produced?
- What other key nutrients do people need?

Engage Your Community
- Buy from local farmers. This can help prevent food from getting ruined because it is shipped long distances.
- Offer nutritious snacks, like fruit and veggies, to your friends.

Change Your Habits
- Read nutrition labels on food packages.
- Eat 'ugly' fruits and veggies. Just because they look funny doesn't mean they taste funny!

Use Your Voice
- Help your family to plan nutritious meals.
- Encourage friends and restaurants to save food rather than throw it away.

Can you come up with other ways to help?

LOCAL

PEOPLE

HEALTH AND HYGIENE

Let's keep ourselves and our communities healthy!

One of the best ways to stay healthy is to avoid getting ill. That is why good **hygiene** habits are important, such as washing your hands with soap and covering your mouth when you cough. Once in a while, germs infect our bodies. **Germs** are tiny things like bacteria and viruses, which can cause **disease** and make us ill.

Our bodies have defence systems to help protect us. Our skin is the first line of protection – it acts like a shield. It is important to clean and cover cuts or scrapes to help keep germs out. What do you need to treat cuts and other injuries? **Make a First Aid Kit that you can take anywhere so that you are always ready!**

Build Your Own First Aid Kit

1) Find a small box with a secure lid or a sturdy sealable bag to hold your kit.
2) Label the container so that you know what it is.
3) Fill your container with:
   - 5-10 adhesive bandages of different sizes
   - Antibacterial ointment
   - Antibacterial wipes or alcohol swabs
   - Hand sanitiser
   - Card with emergency phone numbers (family, doctor, school), a list of your allergies and any other medical conditions

Talk with a grown-up to learn how to use these items and see what else might be useful to include.

Name

Phone

GERMS LIKE TO TRAVEL

Our skin is a great protector, but there are still many ways germs can get into our bodies, like through the nose, mouth and eyes. Germs can be passed in many ways: they can travel in water, be spread through the air when we cough or sneeze, or get transported by insects. We even spread germs to ourselves when we touch our eyes or mouth after touching dirty things.

Sometimes germs spread quickly within a community, making a lot of people ill. This is called an **epidemic**, which can be hard for doctors and nurses to treat and control. Practising good hygiene helps, but when you are ill, it is also important to stay at home and get proper care.

Gather a few friends, put on some clothes you can get dirty and see how quickly germs can spread with this fun activity!

How Do Germs Spread?

You will need:
- Small bowl of powder: flour, baby powder or cornstarch
- Optional: a dark-coloured balloon

Note: you will see the spread of 'germs' better if you wear darker-coloured clothes.

Spread the 'germs'
1) Go outside. Choose 1-2 friends to be 'infected'. They should cover their hands in powder, which represents germs.
2) Interact and play together. For example: shake hands, hug, toss the balloon, open a door, play tag.
3) After 5 minutes, look around. Where do you see powder? Look closely at everyone's hands. Anyone who has powder on his or her hands should go to the bowl and cover them in more powder. Keep playing and see how 'germs' spread.

Clean up
Wash your hands with soap and water. Help to wipe up all the powder and clean your clothes.

Discuss with your friends:
- What actions transferred powder the most?
- What surfaces do you think have lots of germs on them in everyday life?
- How can you help to stop the spread of germs?

STAYING HEALTHY

It can be hard to stay healthy. Some people may not be able to get regular check-ups, go to the doctor when they don't feel well or get the medicines they need. Some may live in places where they do not have clean water for drinking and cooking. In many of these situations, common illnesses such as diarrhoea can become very dangerous.

Learn more about what you can do to stay healthy and what to do when you get ill. **The next time you see your doctor, ask if you can interview him or her.** Be sure to let the doctor's office know you wish to do this when you make your appointment.

Doctor Interview

What do you want to know about keeping you and your community healthy? Here are a few questions to get you started:

When do I need to visit a doctor?

What are the most important things I can do to stay healthy?

What is a **vaccine**? How can it help protect me and my community?

When I am ill, why do you tell me to take medicine sometimes but not others?

Come up with two more questions to ask:

WHAT ELSE CAN YOU DO?

To do all the amazing things we want to do, our bodies need to be healthy. But that's not always easy to accomplish, especially for people living in unhealthy environments or in places where good care is far away. Fortunately, doctors and scientists are discovering more about different diseases and how to treat them. The spread of infectious diseases has dropped as more people practise good hygiene habits and get important medicines.

Even though there has been improvement, people around the world suffer from health problems that could be prevented or treated. Many countries still do not have enough doctors and nurses.

You can help to keep yourself and your communities healthy!
Here are a few ideas to get you started:

Learn More
- How are safe water and sanitation facilities like toilets important for keeping us healthy?
- What are the major infectious diseases in the world?
- What are vaccines and how do they work?

Engage Your Community
- Participate in sports with friends to stay physically active.
- Organise a health fair where people can share tips for staying healthy.

Change Your Habits
- Ask your doctor and dentist how regularly you should visit for a check-up.
- Carry hand sanitiser with you for when there is no soap and water to wash your hands.

Show Kindness
- Give a hug to a friend who looks down. It is important to keep both our minds and bodies healthy!
- If you see someone who is hurt, find out if they need help.

Can you come up with other ways to help?

JOBS AND OPPORTUNITIES

Let's provide people with safe and fair jobs!

Teaching, engineering, farming – these are all **jobs** that people can have. A job provides you with an **income**, or money, to buy what you both need and want. It also provides you with **opportunities** to learn more, meet new people and achieve your dreams.

When more people have jobs, or are **employed**, they help create more products and services that our communities can use and enjoy. Since work is such a big part of our lives, it is important that people are treated well and respected in their jobs.

What should all jobs offer?

Draw a line to match the ideas with what they mean.

FAIR INCOME •

EMPLOYMENT •

SAFE WORK CONDITIONS •

EQUAL OPPORTUNITIES •

JOB SECURITY •

NO CHILD LABOUR •

• Being sure that you will not lose your job

• Getting paid an amount of money that matches the work you do

• Rules and equipment in the workplace that make sure people do not get hurt

• No children are forced to work

• Having a job and getting paid for it

• Having the same chances to learn and grow at work as everyone else

CREATING OPPORTUNITIES

Businesses can create jobs and opportunities for people in the community. A business is a way for people to sell things or provide services in exchange for money. Supermarkets and Internet providers are both examples of businesses.

Entrepreneurs are people who take risks and start businesses. They are taking risks because they do not know if their business will be successful. If you were an entrepreneur, what business would you set up? **Start by making a business plan to tell people about your idea!**

Make a Business Plan

Business name: _____

What will you sell or do?

Who will be your customers?

What tools and supplies will you need? How much will they cost?

How much will your customers pay?

Will you need someone to help?

What will you do with the money you make?

SOPHIE'S DOG WALKING SERVICE

Pitch it!
Share your plan with your friends, family and future customers. Convince them it is a good idea!

29

FAIR TRADE

When you buy items like chocolate bars, what are you actually paying for? The chocolate company uses part of your money to pay for ingredients and part to pay people who help to produce the bar. This includes factory workers, cocoa bean farmers and truck drivers who transport the chocolate.

Sometimes, people work in unsafe workplaces and do not receive a fair price for the work they do. So, how do we support companies that treat workers and farmers well and pay them fairly? Some companies label their products **'fair trade'** to let you know that they are fair to their workers.

Supermarket Scavenger Hunt

Ask a grown-up to take you to a supermarket and see what you can find!

Circle the products that you see with fair trade labels or stickers:

Did you find any other fair trade products? Draw or write about them here:

Draw a fair trade label. Did you find more than one type of label?

Discover the Story

If you buy a fair trade product, see if the label explains fair trade or tells the story of one of the workers who helped to make it.

WHAT ELSE CAN YOU DO?

When more people are employed in good jobs, communities are safer and stronger. That is why many governments are helping to provide better education and training for people. Some businesses are setting up rules to improve working environments and create job opportunities for more people.

However, there are still many people who do not have the right education and training to find good jobs. Some are unemployed and others cannot find jobs that pay enough to take good care of their families. With changes in technology, people also have to learn new skills to keep up.

You can help to provide people with safe and fair jobs!
Here are a few ideas to get you started:

Learn More
- What jobs are most available to people in your community?
- Why are there people who are unemployed in your country?
- What five countries have the highest number of unemployed people?

Engage Your Community
- Set up a career day and invite grown-ups to talk about their jobs.
- Gather friends together and teach each other different skills.

Change Your Habits
- Shop locally to help stores and small businesses in your area.
- Plan out what education and skills you will need to do your dream job.

Use Your Voice
- Ask grown-ups what opportunities there are for them to learn new skills.
- Talk to store owners about fair trade products.

Can you come up with other ways to help?

CITY LIFE

Let's make sure our cities support safe and healthy lives!

Where do you live? Some of us live in the open countryside, but many of us live in large cities. Cities get bigger and busier as more people live in them. Some cities have more than 10 million people living in them! How can a city support all these people?

A city is more than just buildings. A city must also provide many structures and services so that all its people can live healthy lives and work safely together. This includes many useful things: from roads and buses, to sewers and running water, to telephone wires and Internet connection. **Explore some of these services and structures below. Colour each type in a different colour.**

A Colourful City

- **Transportation** helps people to get around.
- **Energy** brings people electricity and power.
- **Communication** helps people to talk and interact.
- **Water** provides people with clean water and takes away dirty water.
- **Waste management** helps people to take care of rubbish and recycling.

PUBLIC TRANSPORTATION

In cities, **public transportation**, like buses and trains, is an important way to help people get around. Public transportation is open to everyone to use. It moves large groups of people at once, which uses less energy than private transportation like cars. So, it can be better for the environment.

Good public transportation can help build strong communities. But in many places, not everyone can enjoy it. Some vehicles are not **accessible**, meaning they are not easy for everyone to use. People may live too far away from stations, or the transportation may not take them to where they need to go.

Have you used public transportation? How can it be made better?

Transportation of the Future

Observe
Take a ride on public transportation and pay attention to:
- What you see, hear, smell and feel
- What people are doing during the ride
- How people get on and off the vehicle

Think
What did you like about the public transportation you observed? What problems did you see?

Design
Design the public transportation of the future! What will you include to make sure that it is accessible for everyone and does not harm our environment? Draw or write about it here:

PUBLIC SPACES

Public spaces in cities are places where everyone can go for free. These include parks, beaches, libraries, city squares and streets. They can be great places for people to relax, play and be entertained. Some of them are also good for the environment. For example, parks are homes to many animals and their trees help to clean the air.

A city provides public spaces and should keep them in good condition. But since we all share these areas, we also share the responsibility to help keep them safe and clean. Has one of your favourite public spaces become dirty lately? **Invite a few friends and a grown-up to help you change that!**

The Big Clean-Up

You will need:
- Rubbish bags
- Protective gloves (like gardening gloves)
- Hand sanitiser

Check out the public space
1) Check with your grown-up to make sure that the space you have chosen is safe to do this activity.
2) Walk around and find an area where people have left litter.

Clean up together
3) Pass out bags and gloves to everyone.
4) Together, decide who will collect rubbish and who will pick up recyclables.
5) Work as a team to collect as much litter as you can.
6) Does the area still look dirty? Ask more people to join if you need help!
7) Once you are done, properly dispose of the rubbish and recycling. Wash your hands thoroughly!

How can we continue to improve our public spaces?

WHAT ELSE CAN YOU DO?

Cities are more than just buildings and transportation. Cities are centres for people to live and work. They are also places to share ideas and cultures. Governments and companies are working together to build and maintain our cities. For example, some of them are building better housing and transportation. Community groups are also coming up with ideas to improve cities for everyone to use.

However, we still have plenty of room to improve. Many cities are poorly designed and maintained. This leads to challenges such as overcrowding, heavy traffic and pollution.

You can help our cities to support safe and healthy lives!
Here are a few ideas to get you started:

Learn More

- What is **urbanisation**?
- What does an **urban planner** do?
- Which five cities in the world have the most people living in them?

Engage Your Community

- Explore your city: visit museums, join events and attend performances.
- Discuss with others how buildings and transportation can be accessed by people with disabilities.

Use Your Voice

- Create a brochure about your favourite city, describing why it is so great. Share it with your family and friends.
- Write a letter to your local leaders telling them what you like about your city and how you would like to improve it.

Show Kindness

- Let people who may need more time, such as the elderly or pregnant women, board a bus or train first.
- Thank someone who works hard to keep your city safe and clean, such as a police officer, bus driver or waste collector.

BEST CITY EVER

Can you come up with other ways to help?

DIVERSITY AND INCLUSION

Let's build communities that value each other's differences!

What really matters about a person? Is it their clothes, weight, voice or age? Sometimes people are treated differently based on their **appearance** or how they look. They may not get the same opportunities as others and may be **excluded**, or left out, from groups or activities.

But people's appearances are just one part of who they are. There is a lot more to people than what you can see.

What do you value in a person? Think about your friends. What is it that makes them special? **Write their characteristics in the spaces below:**

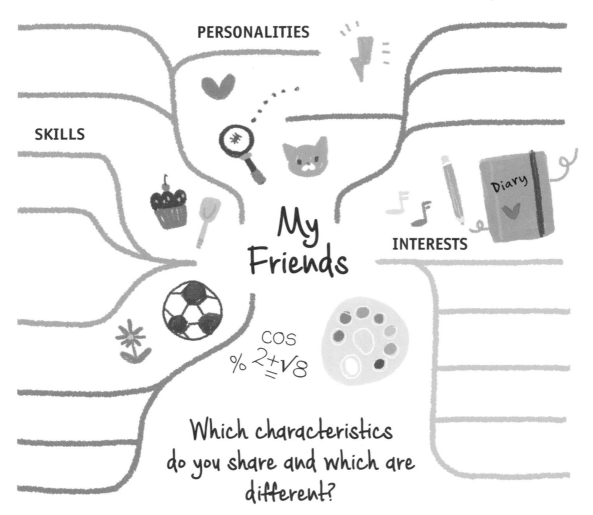

PERSONALITIES

SKILLS

My Friends

INTERESTS

Diary

COS
% $2+\sqrt{8}$

Which characteristics do you share and which are different?

DIVERSITY

People come in many colours and shapes. They are also different in ways that are not always easy to see, like the religion they practise, the people they love, the amount of money they make or the type of education they have received. We call this variety in people **diversity**.

Diversity makes our world more interesting! It means that people have different experiences and ideas. Even though we are all different, we can learn from and relate to each other.

Explore the value of diversity through reading and start a book club with friends!

Diversity Book Club

Book Club Gathering

Getting started

1) One person chooses a book that the whole group will read. The only requirement is that the main character in the story must seem very different from the person who chose the book. For example, the main character could have a different skin colour, a different type of family or come from a different country.

2) Agree upon how much should be read by the next meeting. If it is short, it could be the whole book!

3) How often will you meet? Choose a date and place for your first meeting.

THE HIBOT

Getting together

4) Meet and discuss the story. Think about these questions:
   • How is the main character different from and similar to you?
   • Why does the main character think the way he or she does?
   • Would you act the same way as the main character?
   • What can you learn from the main character's experiences?
   • Come up with other questions to talk about.

5) Decide when to meet next time. Once you finish the story, figure out who will choose the next book!

My Story

GARRY PLOTTER and the Book Swap

INCLUSION

Have you ever been left out? How did that make you feel? It is important that people are not excluded because they seem different. **Inclusion** describes how people come together so that everyone is welcomed and respected. In an inclusive community, people are supported to become the best they can be.

We can make our communities more inclusive by being kind and welcoming to people who seem different from us. We can encourage everyone to participate in activities and decision-making. Sometimes we may need to put in special effort or stand up for others to make sure they are not left out. **Explore ways to be more inclusive by playing the following game with a friend:**

Inclusion Tic-Tac-Toe

1) Each player chooses a symbol: X or O.
2) When you complete an action, draw your symbol over it in the grid below.
3) The first player to complete three actions in a row (down, across or diagonally) is the winner.

Thank someone for making you feel welcomed and included.	During a group discussion, ask the quietest person what he or she thinks.	When you see someone who looks sad, ask how you can help.
Introduce a new type of food to a friend.	At school, join someone who is sitting alone during lunch.	Ask a friend to join you in a new game or sport.
Offer help to someone who is struggling with his or her homework.	During classwork, partner with someone you do not usually work with.	Say good morning to someone you do not usually greet.

Can you complete all the actions?

WHAT ELSE CAN YOU DO?

When we meet people who seem different from us, it is important that we get to understand and respect them. We are all equally important members of our community, so we need to make sure everyone is accepted and respected. People around the world are standing up for groups that are excluded. Governments are creating laws to protect people from being hurt or treated unfairly because they seem different.

But there is still more work to be done. Many groups such as women, people with different skin colours or people with disabilities are often not treated fairly in their daily lives.

**You can help to build communities that value each other's differences!
Here are a few ideas to get you started:**

Learn More

- What is **discrimination**?
- What holidays are celebrated in different parts of the world?
- How diverse are the leaders in your country's government?

Engage Your Community

- Organise a neighbourhood cultural festival. Every family brings traditional food and talks about their culture.
- Find out if your school has rules about inclusion or bullying. If not, work with your head teacher to create some.

Change Your Habits

- Bring together diverse people to work on school projects or games.
- Stand up for people when they are being teased.

Show Kindness

- Let each classmate know why you appreciate him or her.
- Ask someone you do not usually talk to how his or her day is going.

Can you come up with other ways to help?

PEACE AND ORDER

COMMUNITY

Let's create peaceful communities that protect everyone's rights!

There are things that we should all be allowed to do and enjoy freely and equally, no matter who we are, what we believe in or where we come from. These are called our **human rights** and they belong to everyone in the world.

It is important that we and our governments respect and stand up for everyone's human rights. This way we can live together in fair and peaceful communities. **Learn what some of these rights are by decoding them below:**

Know Your Rights

Decoder:
1:A 2:B 3:C 4:D 5:E 6:F 7:G 8:H 9:I 10:J 11:K 12:L
13:M 14:N 15:O 16:P 17:Q 18:R 19:S 20:T 21:U 22:V
23:W 24:X 25:Y 26:Z

$\overline{5}\ \overline{17}\ \overline{21}\ \overline{1}\ \overline{12}\ \overline{9}\ \overline{20}\ \overline{25}$

We are all treated and protected by the law in the same way.

$\overline{12}\ \overline{9}\ \overline{6}\ \overline{5}$

We can all live our lives without fear that someone may take it away.

$\overline{5}\ \overline{4}\ \overline{21}\ \overline{3}\ \overline{1}\ \overline{20}\ \overline{9}\ \overline{15}\ \overline{14}$

We can all learn and go to school.

$\overline{22}\ \overline{15}\ \overline{20}\ \overline{5}$

We can all choose who represents us in the government.

Freedom of $\overline{20}\ \overline{8}\ \overline{15}\ \overline{21}\ \overline{7}\ \overline{8}\ \overline{20}$

We can all have our own beliefs, views and religions.

Freedom of $\overline{19}\ \overline{16}\ \overline{5}\ \overline{5}\ \overline{3}\ \overline{8}$

We can share and express our opinions while respecting others.

40

Can you think of other human rights?

CONFLICTS AND SOLUTIONS

Sometimes people's human rights are taken away during wars. **Wars** happen when countries or large groups of people fight and hurt each other. **Peace** is when people are safe from wars and other violence.

We can all help to create a peaceful community around us. One way is to not fight or hurt others when we face **conflict**, or when we don't get along with each other.

To solve conflicts peacefully it is important that everyone is calm, respectful and listens carefully to others. Then everyone can work together to agree on a good solution.

What does this look like? **See for yourself by creating a comic strip about a conflict.** Show how it could be solved peacefully!

Peaceful Problem-Solving

What is the conflict?	How does each person feel?
What do you say while others listen?	**What do you hear while others talk?**
What solution does everyone agree on?	**What happens next?**

SEEKING SAFETY

One of our human rights is to move to another area to be safe. During wars or after natural disasters, people may need to leave their homes because it is no longer safe for them to stay.

Refugees are people who are forced out of their own countries because of conflicts like wars. They often have to travel long, sometimes dangerous journeys to find safety.

When people are forced to leave their homes, they often cannot carry much with them. After arriving in a new place, they also face many challenges to make their lives as normal as possible.

Imagine if you were forced to leave your country with the activity below:

Pack Your Bags

Pack up
Gather a few friends and at least one grown-up. Ask everyone to do the following:
1) Find a large backpack.
2) Gather things they would take if they were forced to leave their country quickly.
3) Put all of their chosen things in their backpacks. Whatever does not fit must be left behind!

Meet up
Come back together with your backpacks. Share what you packed and discuss:
- What did you choose to take and what did you leave behind? Why?
- What would you miss the most from your home and your country?
- If you ever meet a refugee or someone who lost his or her home, what would you do to show kindness?

What's in your bag?

WHAT ELSE CAN YOU DO?

For communities to live together peacefully, we all need to respect each other's human rights. We also need good governments, fair courts and clear laws to protect our rights. There are human rights organisations around the world, helping to make sure that countries are doing just that.

Some countries help refugees and people who are caught in natural disasters by welcoming them into their country or by sending help. Progress is being made, but there are still many people whose human rights are being taken away because of wars and conflicts.

You can help to create peaceful communities that protect everyone's rights! Here are a few ideas to get you started:

Learn More
- What are other human rights?
- Do children have a different set of human rights?
- Where are some of the major conflicts happening today?

Engage Your Community
- Work with your teacher and classmates to solve problems peacefully by creating a conflict resolution plan at school.
- See if you can visit a place where laws are made, such as a city council or legislature.

Change Your Habits
- Be more aware of what is going on in the world. Try talking with grown-ups or watching the news together.
- Ask people to share their opinions and listen to understand their points of view.

Show Kindness
- Write letters to children who had to leave their homes because of conflicts or disasters.
- Respect and show interest in learning about people's cultures and experiences.

Can you come up with other ways to help?

Dear friend,

I hope you are safe! Stay strong

CLIMATE CHANGE

Let's protect our planet from global warming!

Our Earth's climate is changing – and it is changing fast! **Climate** is the normal weather of an area over a long period of time. Climate change can lead to extreme temperatures. Some places are getting unusually hot while others are getting unusually cold.

Overall, the Earth's climate is getting warmer and warmer. This is called **global warming**. Increasing the Earth's temperature by just 0.5°C can cause serious problems. These changes in climate can lead to natural disasters like bad storms, droughts and floods. Scientists report that ice sheets and glaciers are melting and sea levels are rising. All of this can change or ruin habitats for people, animals and plants.

How could climate change impact the area where you live?

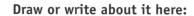

Draw or write about it here:

GREENHOUSE GASES

Climate has changed in the past, but today's climate change is different. This is the first time that people's activities are most likely the main cause. Many scientists think we are creating too many **greenhouse gases (GHGs)**, leading to global warming.

GHGs are all around us, in the air and up in the sky. They keep heat from sunlight closer to Earth, warming it so that living things can survive. But, when there are too many of these gases, they trap too much heat and Earth's temperature rises. This affects the lives of plants, animals and people.

GHGs trap heat just like a blanket. How do you feel when you are covered by a blanket that is too thick and heavy?

Where are all these GHGs coming from?

Find some of the main sources of GHG emissions in the word search below:

```
K L L F O O D W A S T E M I N I N G M L B J R P U
N X Z C A R H L S O R S H R W A V Q I V A L B X D
W Q Z O J N J O Y R P D E F O R E S T A T I O N Z
F V C I U B A I R C O N D I T I O N E R D R O H T
F F N O Q I S X H P W S R Q T V Q R C E P Q I E P
E V Z D E Z R S E C E V D A P R E M O F I Y L L G
R G U Z Z E A E Q B R Y X F S H Y B A O O I G T N
T K B C Z W G R R Q P I X R A B T P L S E I U F H
I Q C O W W W H I A L O S B Q T M A N S K R T J G
L G L N L O V L U F A C T O R Y B F L I S G I U R
I S P T L V M Z Q H N W Q N V R L V P L A N E N X
S I N V V D D Z M D T W N P M L A N D F I L L K R
E I T H W P T L P H T S F H A P U X U U V X T I D
R D F O E M N P I P H Z R S S S I T E E U C K L Q
F H S F N N N O Q Y P C D G K V T J L L Z I W U R
```

CAR • COAL • COW • OIL • FOOD WASTE • PLANE • POWER PLANT • FACTORY
FOSSIL FUEL • MINING • LANDFILL • AIR CONDITIONER • DEFORESTATION
FERTILISER

CARBON FOOTPRINTS

There are many types of GHGs. One of the main ones that humans contribute is carbon dioxide (CO_2). Part of this is natural: when we breathe, we breathe out CO_2. Part of this is not natural: we **emit**, or release, a lot of CO_2 when we produce energy and electricity. Many machines emit other GHGs along with CO_2 into the air.

People can measure their **carbon footprints**, which tells them the amount of GHGs they are adding to the air.

Take this short quiz to get an idea of how big your carbon footprint might be:

1) You tend to eat:
   a) Meat in most meals
   b) Meat in some meals
   c) Little to no meat

2) The light bulbs in your house are:
   a) All traditional bulbs
   b) Some energy-saving bulbs
   c) All energy-saving bulbs

3) You get to school by:
   a) Car
   b) Car-share or public transportation
   c) Bike or foot

4) When you leave your room, you turn off your lights and electronics:
   a) Almost never
   b) Sometimes
   c) All the time

5) If you haven't finished all of your food at the end of a meal, you:
   a) Throw it away
   b) Compost it
   c) Pack it up and eat it later

6) Most of the fresh produce you buy:
   a) Comes from all over the world
   b) Comes from nearby countries
   c) Is local and seasonal

7) If you need to cool your home, you would first try:
   a) Using only air conditioning
   b) Using fans mostly
   c) Opening windows at night and in the morning

8) During your shower, you run warm water for:
   a) 10 minutes or more
   b) 5-10 minutes
   c) 5 minutes or less

Answers

A's: These choices can lead to larger carbon footprints because they emit high amounts of GHGs. What changes can help to lower GHG emissions?

B's: These choices are great ways to begin reducing the size of carbon footprints. Are there more ways to decrease GHG emissions?

C's: These choices help to create small carbon footprints because they use little energy or release low amounts of GHGs. Can you help others to make similar choices?

WHAT ELSE CAN YOU DO?

Many people are unaware of how their everyday actions may contribute to climate change. Climate change affects the whole world and many countries are working together to slow it down. Businesses are developing new technologies such as hybrid and electric cars that emit few GHGs. More people are choosing to cycle or take public transportation, helping to reduce their carbon footprints.

However, global warming continues and we are seeing an increase in natural disasters. Although CO_2 levels are too high, many countries still use fossil fuels like oil for most of their energy needs.

You can help to protect our planet from global warming!
Here are a few ideas to get you started:

Learn More

- What evidence is there that climate is changing?
- How might climate change cause natural disasters like floods?
- What technologies can help us to shrink our carbon footprint, like LED lights?

Engage Your Community

- Get a group together to plant trees and plants. They absorb CO_2 from the air!
- Organise with neighbours to car-share or walk together as a group to school.

Change Your Habits

- Do full loads of laundry and wash clothes in cold water when possible.
- Play more games with toys that do not require electricity.

Use Your Voice

- Help friends to learn about their carbon footprints.
- Start a campaign to help your community reduce GHG emissions.

Can you come up with other ways to help?

CLEAN ENERGY

Let's use the power of clean energy to take care of our planet!

We need energy to make things work. We use it to **generate**, or make, electricity, power our cars and run our cities. Much of our energy comes from burning **fossil fuels** like coal, oil and natural gas. This releases a lot of greenhouse gases (GHGs) and air pollution.

People are starting to use more **clean energy**, which releases little to no GHGs. Clean energy is **renewable** by nature, so it will not run out. The most common types of clean energy are hydropower, wind energy, solar energy and geothermal power. **Fill in the crossword puzzle to learn fun facts about energy!**

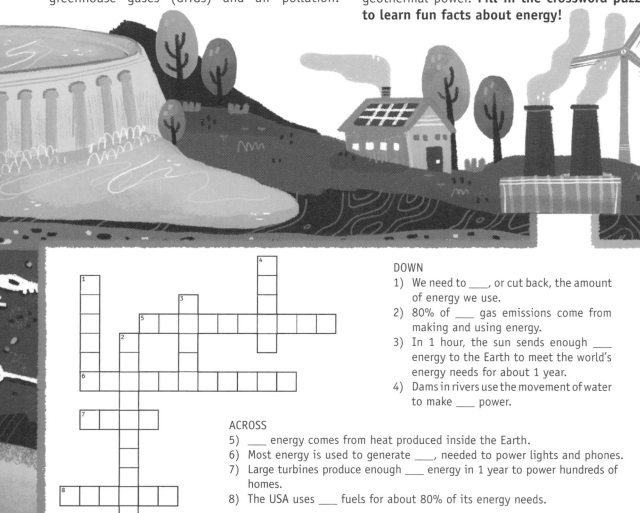

DOWN

1) We need to ___, or cut back, the amount of energy we use.
2) 80% of ___ gas emissions come from making and using energy.
3) In 1 hour, the sun sends enough ___ energy to the Earth to meet the world's energy needs for about 1 year.
4) Dams in rivers use the movement of water to make ___ power.

ACROSS

5) ___ energy comes from heat produced inside the Earth.
6) Most energy is used to generate ___, needed to power lights and phones.
7) Large turbines produce enough ___ energy in 1 year to power hundreds of homes.
8) The USA uses ___ fuels for about 80% of its energy needs.

SOLAR POWER

The sun gives out a lot of energy. Many people think it could become one of our main sources of energy. Solar panels generate electricity from solar energy, which does not release any GHGs or pollute the environment. You can find large solar panels on rooftops or small ones on watches.

Build a solar oven to see the power of the sun for yourself! Be sure to have a grown-up around to help!

Build a Solar Oven

You will need:
- Cardboard box with an attached lid (like a shoe box or pizza box)
- Box-cutter or sharp scissors
- Aluminium foil
- Plastic wrap
- Clear tape
- Black paper
- Rulers or sticks
- Small plate or parchment paper
- Food to heat (avoid raw eggs, fish and meat)

Build your oven
1) Cut a flap out of the box lid. Leave at least a 2.5 cm border around the edge. Wrap the inside of the flap with foil. It should be smooth with the shiny side facing out. Tape it in place.
2) Tightly pull a double layer of plastic wrap over the opening in the lid and tape it in place.
3) Line the bottom of the box with black paper. Tape it in place if needed.
4) Your oven is ready! Use it during the warmest part of the day when the sun is high. Gather your food and head outside.

Heat up your snack
5) Place the oven in a sunny spot, arrange the food on a small plate and place it inside.
6) Close the lid and angle the flap to reflect sunlight into the box. Use a stick to prop it up if needed.
7) Let the sun heat the food. This may take up to an hour depending on how sunny and hot the day is. Check on your oven occasionally to make sure the flap is reflecting the sunlight inside. Be careful when removing plates from your oven – they'll be hot!

Enjoy your snack!

WIND POWER

The wind is powerful. We have used it for ages to move things like sailboats and windmills. Today, large machines called **turbines** capture wind energy. Wind turns the turbine blades, which are connected to a generator to make electricity. Wind energy is a popular clean energy choice because it does not produce air pollution or GHGs.

Like windmills and turbines, pinwheels have blades that turn in the wind.

Make your own pinwheel and see how wind energy works! Grab a grown-up and get started!

Pinwheel Power

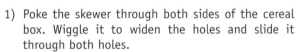

You will need:
- Wooden skewer (Careful – the point can be sharp!)
- Empty cereal box
- 21.5 cm square piece of paper
- Rubber band
- String
- Paper clip
- Scissors
- Tape

1) Poke the skewer through both sides of the cereal box. Wiggle it to widen the holes and slide it through both holes.
2) Wrap a rubber band tightly around the pointed end of the skewer, near where it meets the box. Tie the string around the other end of the skewer. Tie a paper clip to the end of the string.
3) Cut the paper as shown in the diagram.
4) Poke the centre of the paper through the skewer. Bend the left corner of each triangular flap towards the centre and poke it through the skewer, too. Secure the last corner by taping it to one of the other flaps.
5) Blow against the pinwheel and watch the paper clip rise up!

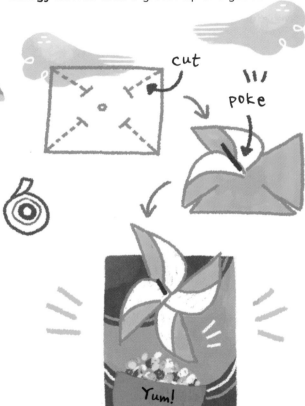

cut

poke

Yum!

Whoosh!
Wind power in action!

WHAT ELSE CAN YOU DO?

Clean energy is renewable and better for our planet. People around the world are finding ways to make clean energy better, easier to get and cheaper to use. For example, solar panels are becoming less expensive and easier to install in homes and buildings. People are becoming more aware of how we consume energy, but we still need to work at reducing our total energy usage. So, why do people still use fossil fuels? Countries tend to use a lot of fossil fuels for heating and transportation. Some types of clean energy require special eqiupment, and some, like geothermal, can only be found in specific places.

**You can help to use the power of clean energy to take care of our planet!
Here are a few ideas to get you started:**

Learn More

- What are the advantages and disadvantages of each type of clean energy?
- What types of clean energy does your country use?
- How much energy does your household use?

Engage Your Community

- Look around your community for evidence of clean energy being used.
- Talk to people about why they do or do not use clean energy.

Change Your Habits

- When it is cold, wear clothing like sweaters to keep warm so that you do not have to heat your home too much.
- Hang your laundry to dry instead of using the dryer.

Use Your Voice

- Present to your class about good energy habits, such as turning out the lights.
- Encourage your community to use more clean energy transportation, like electric buses.

Can you come up with other ways to help?

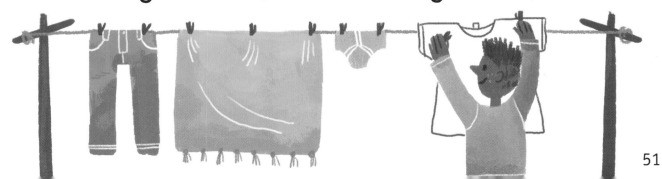

RESOURCES AND WASTE
Let's use our natural resources wisely!

Natural resources are useful things that come from nature. We **consume**, or use, natural resources in many ways. We often use them to produce other things we need, like electricity and food.

Even though the Earth can replace most of its natural resources, it can take a long time.

We have been using our natural resources so quickly that the Earth cannot keep up! When we use these resources, many of our activities produce waste and harm the environment. For example, many cars burn oil or gasoline to move, which also pollutes the air.

What are some ways we use these natural resources?

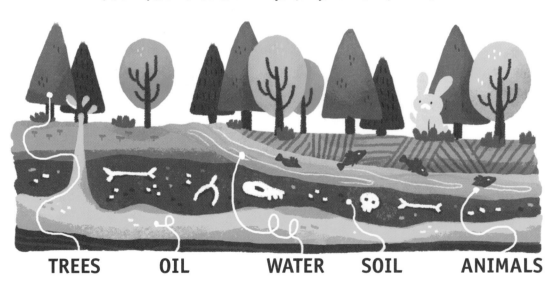

TREES   OIL   WATER   SOIL   ANIMALS

....

....

....

To help keep pressure off the Earth, it is important to **reduce, reuse and recycle.**

REDUCE AND REUSE

Scientists estimate around 80% of the litter in the ocean is **plastic**, like bottles and shopping bags. This pollutes the ocean and makes it hard for life underwater to survive.

It is important to reduce, reuse and recycle materials like plastic and glass because they take a long time to **decompose**, or break down, so that nature can use them again. A plastic bottle can take 450 years to decompose and it can take a simple plastic bag 10-20 years! Reusable bags are an easy way to make a big difference.

Make your own bag by reusing a T-shirt you have outgrown. Find a grown-up to help you with this fun activity.

How long does a glass bottle take to decompose?

Answer: 1 million years!

Make a T-shirt Bag

You will need:
- An old (clean!) T-shirt
- Scissors
- Ruler

Make your bag

1) Cut the sleeves off the T-shirt to make the handles of the bag. Make the cut a little longer than the sleeve hole so that you will be able to slip the handles over your shoulder.
2) Cut out the neck of the shirt to make the opening for your bag.
3) Cut 4 cm long slits 2.5 cm apart along the bottom of the shirt. Hold the front and back of the shirt together when you cut to form matching pairs of strips.
4) Tie each pair of strips tightly together with a double knot.

Ta-da!
Your bag is ready to use.

53

NATURE'S WAY OF RECYCLING

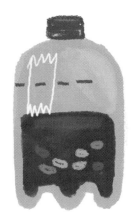

Did you know that most of what comes from nature can be recycled back to nature? Food and garden waste can be **composted**. After the waste decomposes, it can be added to the soil, making it better for plants to grow. Composting is a great way to cut back on your rubbish and grow healthier plants at the same time!

Try your hand at composting. Find a grown-up to help who doesn't mind getting dirty!

Make Your Own Compost

You will need:
- Food scraps (no meat, bones or dairy)
- Garden scraps (like leaves and grass)
- Soil
- Shredded newspaper
- Empty, clean 2L plastic bottle
- Big bucket
- Scissors
- Wide packing tape
- Spray bottle with water

Make your compost
1) Cut all scraps into small pieces, mix with the soil and newspaper in the bucket, and moisten with water.
2) Ask a grown-up to cut open the bottle one third of the way from the top. Leave part of the top attached to form a hinge. Cut two small holes into the bottom of the bottle.
3) Fill the bottle with the mix up to 2.5 cm from the top.
4) Tape the bottle closed and put it in a sunny spot. Roll the bottle each day to mix the 'ingredients'. Keep the mix moist but not wet. Spray it with water or open it to dry when needed.
5) Your compost is ready to add to soil around plants when it looks brown and crumbly. This will take several weeks, so be patient!

Add earthworms to compost faster!

Draw what you observe.

Week 1	Week 2

Week 3	Week 4

WHAT ELSE CAN YOU DO?

To use our natural resources responsibly, we need to reduce what we consume, reuse and recycle when possible. Businesses are creating and using products that can be recycled or decompose easily, like compostable forks. Technology has also helped to reduce how much we consume. For example, using a computer can help us to use less paper.

We still have a lot of work to do to make sure that our resources are around in the future. People produce too much waste, polluting our planet. Important natural resources like clean water can run low in some areas because we are careless in how we consume them.

You can help to use our natural resources wisely!
Here are a few ideas to get you started:

Learn More
- What kind of packaging is least wasteful?
- What is **upcycling**?
- Where does your waste and recycling go?

Engage Your Community
- Make sure there are recycling bins at home, school and public spaces.
- Shop at businesses that produce less waste by using recyclable, compostable or reusable material.

Change Your Habits
- Buy 'loose' food rather than pre-packaged when possible.
- Reuse water: wash veggies in a bowl of water and then give that water to plants.

Use Your Voice
- Make a poster to remind people what goes into the recycling bins.
- Help your family to take care of what they have and only buy what they need.

Can you come up with other ways to help?

PLASTIC   GLASS   PAPER

ENVIRONMENTAL CONSERVATION

Let's protect our natural world!

Look around. What is man-made and what is natural? People can have a big effect on the natural environment. This includes the nonliving parts of nature such as soil and climate, and the living parts such as plants and animals. The living parts are also called **organisms**.

In nature there is a special balance, so that all organisms can get what they need to survive.

Unfortunately, many of our activities are changing this balance. This makes life challenging for many organisms, including ourselves! We have the responsibility to **conserve**, or repair and protect, nature. This way, we can all can live together and enjoy nature now and in the future.

Find a path to clean oceans and healthy lands by avoiding some of the activities that harm the environment!

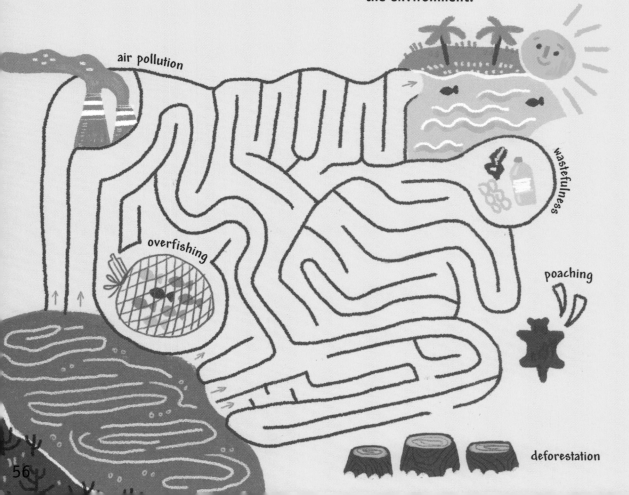

air pollution

wastefulness

overfishing

poaching

deforestation

56

Did you know that oceans cover almost ¾ of the Earth and are home to possibly over 1 million different types of organisms? No wonder they provide many natural resources we use for food, medicine and energy!

The high amount of CO_2 in the air is changing our climate and our oceans, too! Oceans absorb CO_2. The more they absorb, the more acidic they become. This is called **ocean acidification**, and it can make life difficult for ocean organisms. For example, it can affect coral growth and the ability of some animals, like clams and crabs, to build their shells.

Discover what ocean acidification can do to the shells of animals by observing the effects of acid on an eggshell!

Ocean Acidification

You will need:
- Water
- White vinegar
- 3 jars or glasses
- 1 eggshell broken into equally sized pieces

1) Fill one jar halfway up with water.
2) Fill the next jar halfway up with equal amounts of water and vinegar.
3) Fill the last jar halfway up with only vinegar.
4) Place equal amounts of eggshell in each jar. Do you notice a reaction?
5) Cover the jars and check on them twice a day for a few days. What happened to the shells in each jar?
6) The ocean is not as acidic as vinegar, but it is slowly becoming more acidic. How do you think this will affect the growth of coral and shells of animals like oysters or clams?

OUR LANDS

From tiny ants to tall giraffes, life on land takes many interesting and beautiful forms. Life is found in all sorts of different environments, from dry deserts to colourful rainforests to icy tundras.

Every environment has important natural resources that organisms need to survive. For example, beavers need trees and clean streams to build their homes. What might happen to organisms if the natural resources they depend on run out or become polluted?

Nature is full of wonders that must be cared for and protected. **Discover its treasures near you and share what you find with friends and family!**

footprints

I ♥ Nature!

Nature's Treasures

You will need:
- Pencil and paper and/or a camera

1) Invite a grown-up to go with you to explore some nature nearby. This could be a nature preserve, a park, a garden or even a green space in your city.
2) Walk around. Write, draw or take pictures of:
   - different plants and animals
   - resources that plants and animals need to survive
   - clues that animals have been there
3) Find a spot to stop and sit. Make no noise for 5 minutes (try closing your eyes). Note down what you heard and how you felt.

4) Think about the following:
   - What are some of nature's treasures?
   - Is anything disrupting the environment, such as litter or loud noise? Can you do anything about it?
5) Gather your pictures and thoughts together. Display them on a wall, set them up on a table or create a poster to show friends and family. Share what you learned. Ask others why they value nature and why it is important to conserve it.

WHAT ELSE CAN YOU DO?

The Earth is a beautiful place with millions of types of animals and plants. Many of our activities throw off the balance of natural resources and organisms we find in nature. However, people are becoming more aware of the effect we can have on the environment and are working together to conserve it.

Governments have created laws to limit pollution, and more areas on land and in the oceans are becoming specially protected. But there is still a lot of work to be done. Cutting down forests, overfishing and pollution continue to be problems. More organisms, like coral, are close to becoming extinct.

You can help to protect our natural world! Here are some ideas to get you started:

Learn More

- What other human activities are affecting the environment?
- What is an **ecosystem**?
- What is being done to protect **endangered** animals?

Engage Your Community

- Spend time in nature with friends. You could hike, go to the beach or birdwatch!
- Join or organise activities with your community on Earth Day (22nd April).

Donate and Volunteer

- Hold a cake sale and raise money for an organisation that protects endangered animals.
- Join a coastal clean-up day and help to keep litter out of our oceans.

Change Your Habits

- Check that the seafood you buy is a healthy choice for you and the oceans.
- Avoid using single-use plastic products, like straws, which end up polluting oceans and the land.

Can you come up with other ways to help?

JUST THE BEGINNING

Creative and caring people like you are just what we need to take on global challenges and improve our world! There are many ways that you can make a difference.

This book is just the beginning. Global challenges will keep changing, so we all need to be ready to learn and find new ways to help.

You can start with changing your own habits, volunteering or donating to those in need. And remember, showing kindness can go a long way! By working together, we can accomplish so much more. So, use your voice and engage your community to improve our world.

**Remember, small changes with just one person
can grow into big changes with a lot of people.**

Let's all help to make the world a better place!

ANSWER KEY

Chapter 3: Hunger and Nutrition
What are some of the key nutrients we need each day?
1) carbohydrates
2) protein
3) good fats
4) iron
5) vitamin D
6) calcium

Chapter 5: Jobs and Opportunities
What should all jobs offer?

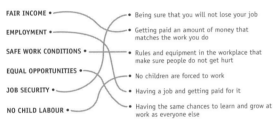

FAIR INCOME • → • Getting paid an amount of money that matches the work you do

EMPLOYMENT • → • Having a job and getting paid for it

SAFE WORK CONDITIONS • → • Rules and equipment in the workplace that make sure people do not get hurt

EQUAL OPPORTUNITIES • → • Having the same chances to learn and grow at work as everyone else

JOB SECURITY • → • Being sure that you will not lose your job

NO CHILD LABOUR • → • No children are forced to work

Chapter 6: City Life
A Colourful City
1) Transportation: roads, train and train station
2) Energy: solar panels and wind turbine
3) Communications: network tower, satellite dish and antenna
4) Water: water treatment plant and river
5) Waste management: recycling station and rubbish bin (next to the train station!)

Chapter 8: Peace and Order
Know Your Rights
1) equality
2) life
3) education
4) vote
5) thought
6) speech

Chapter 9: Climate Change

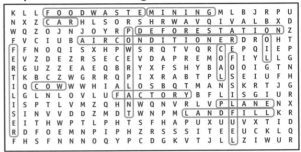

Chapter 10: Clean Energy

Chapter 11: Resources and Waste
What are some ways we use these natural resources?
Here are some examples:
- Trees: to produce paper and furniture
- Oil: for heating buildings and fueling cars
- Water: for drinking and washing laundry
- Soil: to grow crops and support organisms
- Animals: for food and to make clothing

Chapter 12: Environmental Conservation

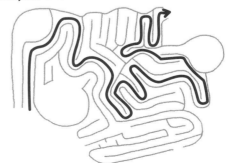

REFERENCES AND RESOURCES

Overviews of Global Challenges from the United Nations
UN Sustainable Development Goals: facts, figures and flyers about each goal
[http://www.un.org/sustainabledevelopment/sustainable-development-goals/]
UN Sustainable Development Knowledge Platform: summaries of targets, progress, and indicators
[https://sustainabledevelopment.un.org/sdgs]

Extreme Poverty
Dollar Street: collection of photos from different countries, sorted by income level
[https://www.gapminder.org/dollar-street/matrix]
Plan International: examples of causes and ways to break the cycle of poverty
[https://plancanada.ca/cycle-of-poverty]
World Bank's Poverty Data Portal: database of poverty indicators around the world
[http://povertydata.worldbank.org/poverty/home]

Hunger and Nutrition
Food and Agricultural Organization of the UN: food waste facts, videos and links to more resources
[http://www.fao.org/food-loss-and-food-waste/en/]
Healthy Kids Association: guides on nutrients and healthy eating; includes content designed for children, parents and teachers [https://healthy-kids.com.au/food-nutrition/nutrients-in-food/]
World Food Programme: current information on the causes and state of global hunger and malnutrition
[http://www1.wfp.org/zero-hunger]

Health and Hygiene
World Health Organization: resource and database on global health issues [http://www.who.int/]
healthychildren.org: guidelines, articles and tips about children's health [https://www.healthychildren.org]
American Red Cross: a how-to guide for an adult's first aid kit
[http://www.redcross.org/get-help/how-to-prepare-for-emergencies/anatomy-of-a-first-aid-kit]

Universal Education
Global Education Monitoring Report: 2016 report on world barriers and progress to achieving quality education for all
[http://unesdoc.unesco.org/images/0024/002457/245752e.pdf]
The World Bank: facts and multimedia resources about girls' education
[http://www.worldbank.org/en/topic/girlseducation]
Global Citizen: overviews of common barriers to education
[https://www.globalcitizen.org/en/content/10-barriers-to-education-around-the-world-2/]

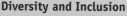

Diversity and Inclusion
The Barefoot Mommy: activities and book lists curated around different countries and cultures
[http://www.thebarefootmommy.com/category/global-kids/]
Playworks: game library with many fun and inclusive games across different age groups
[https://www.playworks.org/game-library/]
Stop Bullying: ways for schools, adults and children to prevent and stop bullying [https://www.stopbullying.gov/]

City Life
Metropolis: A Green City of Your Own!: curriculum to learn about different elements of a city
[https://www.planning.org/publications/document/9149250/]
A Kid's Guide to Building Great Communities: exercises to learn about urban planning and community development
[https://www.cip-icu.ca/Files/Resources/kidsguide.aspx]
101 Small Ways You Can Improve Your City: communities can all get involved in these ideas
[https://www.curbed.com/2016/9/22/13019420/urban-design-community-building-placemaking]

Peace and Justice
UN Convention on the Rights of the Child: child-friendly resources explaining children's rights and responsibilities
[https://www.unicef.org/rightsite/484_540.htm]
Kids Matter: tips to help children resolve conflict at home
[https://www.kidsmatter.edu.au/families/enewsletter/helping-children-resolve-conflict]
UNHCR Teaching about Refugees: classroom resources that can be adapted for use at home
[http://www.unhcr.org/uk/teaching-about-refugees.html]

Jobs and Opportunities
International Labour Organization: detailed explanation of the Decent Work Agenda
[http://www.ilo.org/global/topics/decent-work/]
Lemonade Day: resources to teach children how to start their own businesses [https://lemonadeday.org/resources]
Fairtrade Schools: activities and resources to learn about fair trade, sorted by age [https://schools.fairtrade.org.uk/resource/]

Climate Change
A Student's Guide to Global Climate Change: child-friendly climate change lessons, activities and tools like a carbon footprint calculator (the adult version of this site is useful, too!)
[https://www3.epa.gov/climatechange//kids/index.html]
NASA Climate Kids: climate change information, activities and games for children (the adult version of this site is useful, too!) [https://climatekids.nasa.gov]
Climate Communication: videos, articles and educational resources on climate change
[https://www.climatecommunication.org/]

Clean Energy
Energy.gov: renewable energy trends, US energy consumption reports and energy-saving tips [https://www.energy.gov/]
European Commission: EU actions and reports on energy and climate change
[https://ec.europa.eu/clima/policies/international/paris_protocol/energy_en]
National Geographic: articles and facts about clean energy sources, climate change and the environment
[https://www.nationalgeographic.com/]

Natural Resources
National Institute of Environmental Health Sciences: child-friendly explanations about waste, and tips on how to reduce, reuse and recycle [https://kids.niehs.nih.gov/topics/reduce/index.htm]
California Academy of Sciences: a natural resource BINGO game; includes links to additional resources
[https://www.calacademy.org/educators/lesson-plans/natural-resources-bingo]
Marine Debris Program: describes how litter affects oceans; includes posters, activities and curricula for children
[https://marinedebris.noaa.gov/]

Environmental Conservation
National Geographic Kids: child-friendly information, games and videos about the environment and animals
[https://kids.nationalgeographic.com/]
Pacific Marine Environmental Laboratory: explanation of ocean acidification with links to data and research studies
[https://www.pmel.noaa.gov/co2/story/Ocean+Acidification]
UN Environment: explores environmental threats; includes current news, stories and suggestions to get involved
[https://www.nature.org/ourinitiatives/urgentissues/land-conservation/index.htm]

ABOUT US

Karen Ng (Co-Author)

Karen grew up in Hong Kong, where she spent her childhood playing tag in parks, losing herself in books and caring for her pet hamsters.

After starting her career as an investment banking analyst, she now works in social impact investing, helping people and organisations to invest their money in a way that creates positive change in the world.

She holds an MBA from the University of Oxford and a BSc in Government and Economics from the London School of Economics. She lives with her husband in London, where she volunteers for local women's and refugees' charities, two causes that are very close to her heart.

Kirsten Liepmann (Co-Author)

Kirsten grew up exploring different cultures and parts of the globe. She spent time living in Germany, Puerto Rico, Spain, Japan and the USA – all before she turned nineteen. After earning a BA from Dartmouth College and an MS in Education from Northwestern University, she taught in elementary school for seven years before obtaining an MBA from the University of Oxford.

She believes that education and children are the key to positive change and currently works in an education nonprofit in San Jose, California.

When she has time, she will take off to enjoy nature, and when she has a little less time, she will stay in to bake treats for friends and family.